Edited by Only Pop Fans

Written and drawn by Kev F Sutherland

@KevFComicArtist

kevfcomicartist.com

First published in Great Britain in 2021 by
UT Productions Ltd
10 St Ann St
Chepstow
NP16 5HE

Copyright ©2021 Kev F Sutherland

kevfcomicartist.com
Twitter & Facebook: @KevFComicArtist

Kev F Sutherland has asserted his right under the
Copyright, Designs and Parent Act 1988 to be
identified as the author of this work

All rights reserved. No part of this publication may be
reproduced, stored in a retrieval system, or transmitted
in any form or by any means, without the
prior permission of the publishers

This is a work of fiction. All the characters and events portrayed
in this book are fictional, and any resemblance to real people
or incidents is purely coincidental

British Library Cataloguing-in-Publication Data
A catalogue record for this book is available from the British Library

Eurovision

The Eurovision Song Contest began life in 1956 as a songwriting competition, bringing the nations of Europe together in a spirit of creative collaboration and gentle competition.

The number of countries has grown, from just seven in the first competition, to 22 by 1990. In 2021, 39 countries took part, with a pair of semi finals taking place during the week, before the grand final on the Saturday night.

As the years have progressed, the styles of music have changed, sometimes in stark parallel to the music that was actually in the pop charts back home. For a few years, as rock and roll was dominating the radio, the songs were very traditional and old fashioned ballads. The first hint of choreography of any sort was when 1958's entry from Italy raised his arms slightly. It wasn't until 1965 that a recognisable pop song, written as it happens by Serge Gainsbourg, was entered in the contest, much to the annoyance of traditionalists who thought this was the beginning of the end. It wasn't.

The voting has always been an interesting part of the night. Sometimes riveting, sometimes boring, sometimes going on forever, but regularly changing. After a four way tie in 1969 the rules changed a little. When phone voting from home came in, results started to reflect national tastes better, but also threw up the anomalies of countries who would vote for each other regardless of the song.

As the years have progressed, the efforts made by contestants to represent their songs visually has come on so far that, at times, the look overwhelms the song itself. When Brotherhood Of Man did a bit of innocent skirt-whipping-off, they had no idea what they'd started. If only this book could do justice to them. But, until you colour the pages in, it's only halfway there.

There are bound to be dozens of acts you wish were in this book, and they're not there cos we only had room for 33 and a third (you can guess which one's the third). If this book proves popular, hopefully a second book will fill in those gaps.

Being written from a British and Irish perspective, you'll notice there are a few acts you, reading this in Europe or Australia, may not have chosen. Forgive us our Cliff Richards, Jedwards, and Johnny Logans, and sorry if they elbowed out your personal favourite.

Happy colouring

Kev F Comic Artist

Lys Assia

Lys Assia will one day win you a pub quiz, or a round of Only Connect, when you remember that, in 1956, she was the winner of the very first Eurovision Song Contest. Held in Lugano, Switzerland, this first contest had only 7 competing countries – Belgium, France, Germany, Italy, Luxembourg, Netherlands, and the winners, and hosts, Switzerland. The UK made their debut in the contest the following year.

Domenico Modugno

Italy's Eurovision third-placed song from 1958 is in fact called Nel Blu Depinto De Blu, but is far better known from its chorus of Volare. Singer Domenico executed the first bit of Eurovisual choreography when he raised his arms on that line. Tame, but it had the desired effect.

France Gall

France Gall's 1965 winning song for Luxembourg, Poupee De Cire Poupee De Son, was written by Serge Gainsbourg. It was so popular she went on to record versions in German, Italian, and Japanese, but not one in English. That was eventually recorded by Twinkle as A Lonely Singing Doll.

Sandie Shaw

Wearing no shoes, her USP throughout her pop career, Sandie Shaw's winning entry in 1967 was Britain's first. Her song, Puppet On A String, was chosen from five shortlisted numbers which she performed on the Rolf Harris Show.

Cliff Richard

Cliff has represented the UK at Eurovision twice, with 1968's Congratulations coming second by just one point, and 1974's Power To All My Friends coming third. The 1968 contest was the first to be broadcast in colour, in those countries that had the technology, and was presented by regular mutil-lingual host Katie Boyle.

©2022 Kev F Sutherland kevfcomicartist.com

Lulu

1969's Eurovision Song Contest results led to a change in the voting system after there was a four way tie at the top. Lulu's Boom Bang A Bang got the same score as the entries from Spain, The Netherlands, and France, and all four countries shared the prize.

Dana

Dana Rosemary Scallon was only 19 when she won Eurovision for Ireland in 1970 with All Kinds Of Everything. She went on to serve as an Irish Member of the European Parliament from 1999 to 2004.

ABBA

Failing to qualify for Sweden in 1973 with their song Ring Ring, with English lyrics translated by Neil Sedaka, the four piece from Sweden had better luck second time round. Their 1974 winner Waterloo is repeatedly voted Best Eurovision Winner Ever.

Brotherhood of Man

Formed as an umbrella group with a changeable roster, by songwriter Tony Hiller, the settled line up of Martin Lee, Lee Sheriden, Nicky Stevens and Sandra Stevens won Eurovision in 1976 with Save Your Kisses For Me before going on to a succession of chart hits in the UK.

Jahn Teigen

1978's Norwegian entry, Mille Etter Mille, made Eurovision history when, under the voting system that had been in place since 1970, it was the first song to receive the dreaded Nul Points. Undaunted, Jahn Tiegen went on to represent his country again in 1982 and 1983, having attempted to enter the contest 16 times.

Terry Wogan

Between 1971 and 2008, Terry Wogan was the BBC's commentator in the Eurovision Song Contest, either on TV or radio, even on occasion combing the role of on-stage presenter and off-screen voice over. His amusing but irreverent comments were not received well by some countries but became a staple of the show in the UK and his native Ireland. His tradition has been maintained since by Graham Norton.

Johnny Logan

Famously the only artist to have won Eurovision twice, in 1980 and 1987, Johnny also went on to write the winning song Why Me, for Linda Martin in 1992. These are three of Ireland's record breaking seven wins, which include being the only country to win for three consecutive years.

©2022 Kev F Sutherland kevfcomicartist.com

Buck's Fizz

The Fizz's winning song for the UK in 1981, Making Your Mind Up, was written by Andy Hill who went on to co write most of their subsequent singles, as well as hits for lots of artists including Celine Dion, Westlife, Cliff Richard and Cher.

Sandra Kim

In more recent years of the contest, Sandra Kim wouldn't have been eligible to compete because, when she won for Belgium in 1986 singing J'aime La Vie, she was only 13 years old. When this led to a trend of ever younger entrants, with 1989's contest including acts aged 11 and 12, the rules were amended so that, since 1990, all performers must be over the age of 16. The Junior Eurovision Song Contest began in 2003, by popular demand. From sharp elbowed parents, if not from viewers.

Celine Dion

Canadian Celine won Eurovision in 1988 singing Ne Partez Pas Sans Moi for Switzerland, in French. It was written by Turkish composer Atilla Sereftug and Swiss lyricist Nelly Martinetti. To date it is the last French language song to win the contest. Since then Celine has gone onto international stardom, eclipsing her predecessors Abba as the most successful and longest-running recording artist to have competed in Eurovision.

Riverdance

Not an entry in the contest itself, this piece of music by the composer Bill Whelan was accompanied by a dance routine choreographed and performed by Irish dancing champions Michael Flatley and Jean Butler, and troupe, in the voting interval of the 1994 Eurovision Song Contest in Dublin, and has remained more memorable than almost any act in the show. Except of course for that year's winner, which was of course... er, ok, so Riverdance was the only memorable thing in the show.

Katrina and the Waves

Well known for their hit Walking On Sunshine, Kansas native Katrina Leskanich and her British band, led by songwriter Kimberly Rew, won Eurovision for the UK in 1997 with Love Shine A Light.

Dana International

Sharon Cohen, aka Dana International, has had a string of hit albums in her native Israel, and won Eurovision in 1998 with the rousing anthem Diva, which namechecks Aphrodite, Cleopatra, and Victoria.

Jemini

Liverpool's Chris Crosby and Gemma Abbey achieved notoriety in 2003, becoming the first UK act to receive the dreaded Nul Points for their song Cry Baby. Since then only two more countries have received this low a score, both in 2015: Germany and, that year's host country, Austria.

Lordi

Formed in Finland in 1992 by Tomi Petteri Putaansuu, aka Mr Lordi, this heavy rock band with their unforgettable Halloween horror make up won Eurovision in 2002 with Hard Rock Hallelujah

Verka Serduchka

Andriy Mykhailovych Danylko, known for their drag persona Verka Seduchka, is a Ukrainian comedian who only came second in 2007 with the song Dancing Lasha Tumbai, which earns its place in this book on visual appeal alone.

Alexander Rybak

Belarusian-Norwegian singer-composer, violinist, pianist and actor Alexander Rybak won Eurovision for Norway in 2009 with Fairytale, characterised by his virtuoso violin playing, while singing and dancing live.

Loreen

Looking like Claudia Winkleman in a wind tunnel, Lorine Zineb Nora Talhaoui won Eurovision for Sweden in 2012 singing Euphoria. The song received the highest number of maximum points of any entry in the contest's history with eighteen countries giving the song their top marks.

Jedward

Of all Ireland's entrants in Eurovision, including a record seven wins, why would we include a pair of twins who didn't even win when they were the country's representatives in 2011, coming 19th? Because look at them and tell us they aren't the best looking thing in this book.

Conchita Wurst

Thomas Neuwirth, aka drag queen Conchita, was a founding member of boy band Jetz Anders, having won the talent show Starmania. Their solo anthem Rise Like A Phoenix won Eurovision for Austria in 2014

Mans Zelmerloew

Winning 2015's Eurovision for Sweden with Heroes, accompanied by impressive cartoon animation, Mans went on to co-host the following years contest. He had previously won the first season of Let's Dance, the Swedish version of Strictly Come Dancing.

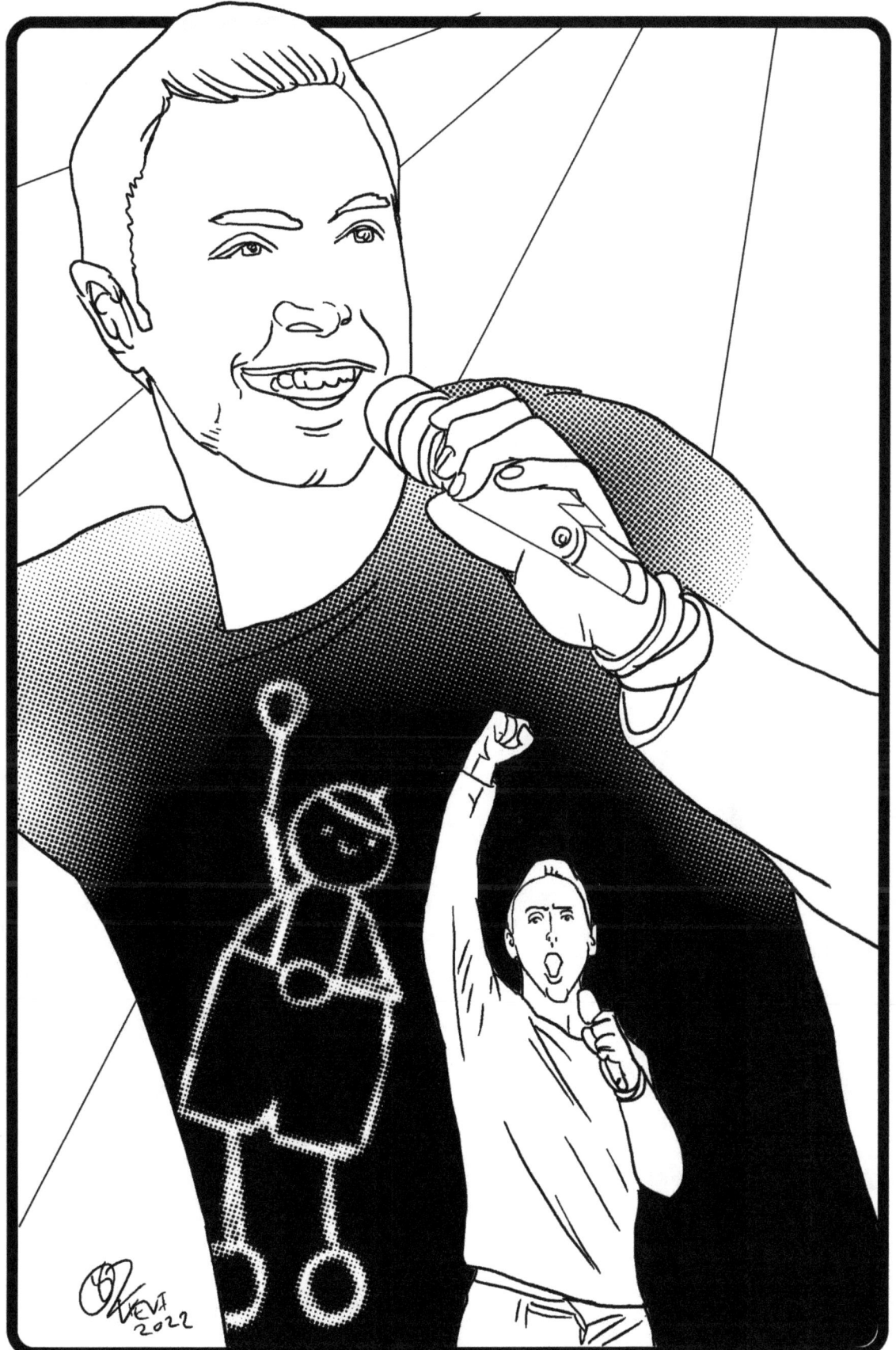

Jamala

1944 by Jamala won the 2016 Eurovision Song Contest for Ukraine, and is the first entry to have been sung in the Crimean language. Eurovision rules prohibit lyrics that could be interpreted as having political content, but in interviews at the time Jamala made it clear that her song was sung in protest at the recent Russian annexation of Crimea, a conflict which is continuing.

Keiino

Norwegian supergroup Keiino feature Fred-Rene Buljo, who raps in the Finno-Urgic language of the Sami people. Their song, Spirit In The Sky, only came 6th in the 2019 final, despite its unique and unforgettable yoiking segment, a Sami singing style which mimics the sounds of nature, making the Arctic Circle sound well worth steering clear of.

Eleni Fouriera

Greece's Entala Fureraj, as Eleni Fouriera, represented Cyprus in 2018's contest with the song Fuego, coming second in the grand final. Her hair flick remains one of the best beloved images of the contest. Since the advent of televoting in 1998, Greece and Cyprus have consistently given each other the full marks of twelve points, expect once in 2015, for no obvious reason. It is loudly, but good-naturedly, jeered every time it happens.

Netta

Netta Barzalai won in 2018 singing Toy, having auditioned for Hakakhov Haba, the Israel song selection show, singing the Spice Girls' Wannabe, and a mashup of Gangnam Style and Tik Tok.

This was Israel's fourth win in the contest, in which it has participated since 1973 despite not, geographically, being part of Europe. Since we started letting Australia take part, this hasn't been mentioned so much.

Kate Miller-Heidke

Australia were first invited to enter the Eurovision Song Contest in 2015, because of the country's love of the contest, and not because something devastating and horrifying had happened to the tectonic plates of the planet moving it from the other side of the planet to the Mediterranean. To date their most outstanding entry is undoubtedly Kate Miller-Heidke, a classically trained singer who performed, in an operatic soprano voice, while balancing at the top of a forty foot pole. Though only coming 9th in the 2019 final, her performance remains one of Eurovision's most visually impressive.

Daði Freyr and Gagnamagnið

Icelandic singer Daði and his band were due to represent Iceland at the 2020 Eurovision song contest which was, of course, cancelled because of the Covid 19, and were anticipated to be likely winners with their comedic song Think About Things. Like most of the 2020 line up, they took the chance to represent their country again in 2021, this time singing 10 Years, which finished in fourth place.

©2022 Kev F Sutherland   kevfcomicartist.com

Fire Saga

Hailing from the small town of Husavik in Iceland, childhood friends Lars Eriksson and Sigrit Eriksdóttir wanted nothing more than to represent their country at Eurovision, being best known for the locally popular hit Ja Ja Ding Dong. In 2020, having failed to win the qualifying contest, they were lucky enough to be the only survivors of a boat explosion which killed every other contestant and so were able to represent Iceland singing Double Trouble, featuring a dance routine in a hamster wheel.

Maneskin

Their name meaning moonlight in Italian, Maneskin followed their 2021 win with Zitti E Buoni by becoming the first Italian rock band to have a top ten single in the UK with the follow up, I Wanna Be Your Slave.

Shakespeare graphic novels
by Kev F Sutherland

Midsummer Night's Dream Team
Quince gets the gang together for one last job. Shakespeare's comedy as a heist movie.

The Prince Of Denmark Street
Hamlet & The Danes are a punk rock band in the 1970s.

Findlay Macbeth
Fife, 1977, social climbing with lots of deaths. The Scottish Play meets Abigail's Party.

All available on Amazon and Kindle Unlimited
Signed copies from kevfcomicartist.com

Printed in the USA
CPSIA information can be obtained
at www.ICGtesting.com
LVHW081450111223
766205LV00005B/570